Already the slim crocus stirs the snow,
And soon yon blanched fields will bloom again
With nodding cowslips for some lad to mow,
For with the first warm kisses of the rain,
The winter's icy sorrow breaks to tears,
And the brown thrushes mate,
And with bright eyes the rabbit peers
From the dark warren where the fir cones lie,
And treads one snowdrop underfoot, and runs
Over the mossy knoll, and blackbirds fly
Across our path at evening, and the suns
Stay longer with us; ah, how good to see
Grass-girdled Spring in all her joy of laughing greenery!

Oscar Wilde

ISBN 0-8249-1025-7 350

IDEALS—Vol. 41. No. 2 February MCMLXXXIV IDEALS (ISSN 0019-137X) is published eight times a year,
February, March, April, June, August, September, November, December
by IDEALS PUBLISHING CORPORATION 11315 Watertown Plank Road, Milwaukee, Wis. 53226
Second class postage paid at Milwaukee, Wisconsin and additional mailing offices.
Copyright © MCMLXXXIV by IDEALS PUBLISHING CORPORATION.
POSTMASTER: Send address changes to Ideals, Post Office Box 2100, Milwaukee, Wis. 53201
All rights reserved. Title IDEALS registered U.S. Patent Office.
Published simultaneously in Canada.

ONE YEAR SUBSCRIPTION—eight consecutive issues as published—$15.95
TWO YEAR SUBSCRIPTION—sixteen consecutive issues as published—$27.95
SINGLE ISSUE—$3.50
Outside U.S.A., add $4.00 per subscription year for postage and handling

Publisher, Patricia A. Pingry
Editor/Ideals, Kathleen S. Pohl
Managing Editor, Marybeth Owens
Art Director, David Schansberg
Production Manager, Mark Brunner
Photographic Editor, Gerald Koser
Copy Editor, Barbara L. Nevid
Research Editor, Geraldine Zisk

*Front and
back cover
Fred Sieb*

Light

From "Paradise Lost," Book VII

"Let there be light," God said; and forthwith
  Light
Ethereal, first of things, quintessence pure,
Sprung from the deep; and from her native east
To journey through the aery gloom began,
Sphered in a radiant cloud, for yet the Sun
Was not; she in a cloudy tabernacle
Sojourned the while. God saw the light was
  good;
And light from darkness by the hemisphere
Divided: light the Day, and darkness Night,
He named.

Milton

Mariposa Lily

Insect or blossom? Fragile, fairy thing,
Poised upon slender tip and quivering
To flight! a flower of the fields of air,
A jeweled moth, a butterfly with rare
And tender tints upon his downy wing,
A moment resting in our happy sight,
A flower held captive by a thread so slight;
Its petal-wings of broidered gossamer
Are light as the wind, with every wind astir,
Wafting sweet odor, faint and exquisite.
O dainty nursling of the field and sky,
What fairer thing looks up to heaven's blue
And drinks the noontide sun, the dawning's dew?
Thou winged bloom! thou blossom-butterfly!

Ina Donna Coolbrith

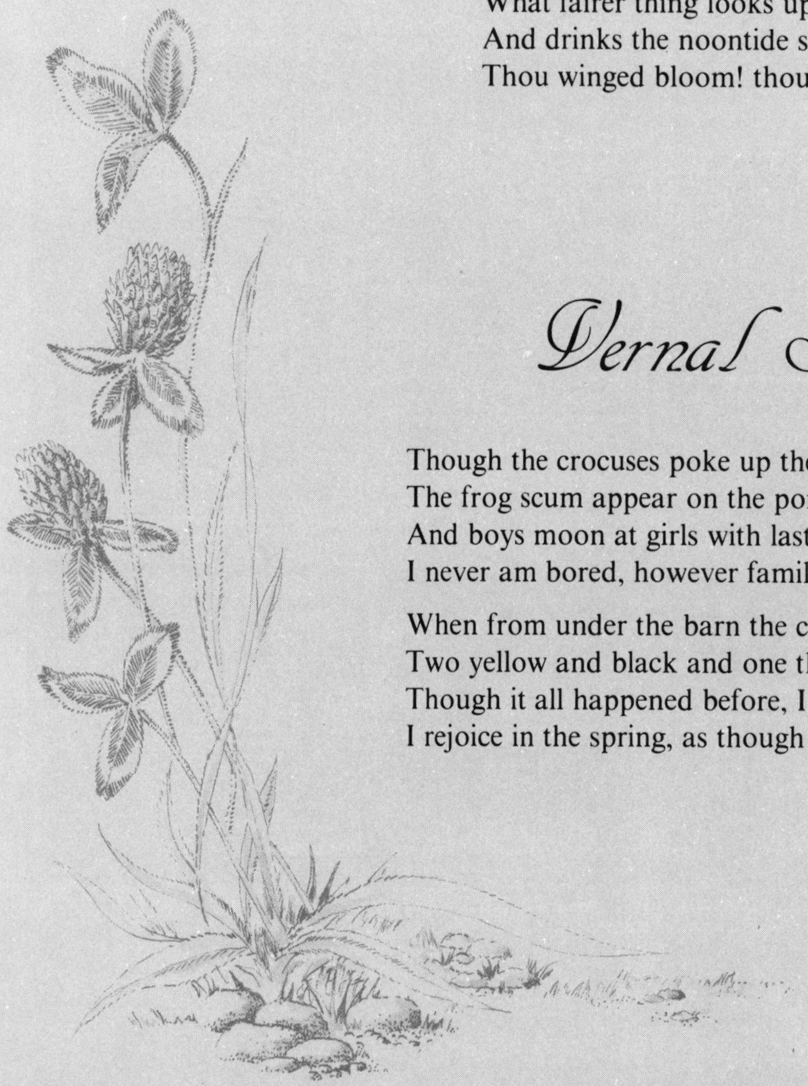

Vernal Sentiment

Though the crocuses poke up their heads in the usual places,
The frog scum appear on the pond with the same froth of green,
And boys moon at girls with last year's fatuous faces,
I never am bored, however familiar the scene.

When from under the barn the cat brings a similar litter—
Two yellow and black and one that looks in between—
Though it all happened before, I cannot grow bitter;
I rejoice in the spring, as though no spring ever had been.

Theodore Roethke

As a child looks forward to the coming of the summer, so could we contemplate with quiet joy the circle of the seasons returning without fail eternally. As the spring came round during so many years of the gods, we could go out to admire and adorn anew our Eden, and yet never tire.

Henry David Thoreau

A Prayer in Spring

Oh, give us pleasure in the flowers today;
And give us not to think so far away
As the uncertain harvest; keep us here
All simply in the springing of the year.

Oh, give us pleasure in the orchard white,
Like nothing else by day, like ghosts by night;
And make us happy in the happy bees,
The swarm dilating round the perfect trees.

And make us happy in the darting bird
That suddenly above the bees is heard,
The meteor that thrusts in with needle bill
And off a blossom in midair stands still.

For this is love, and nothing else is love;
The which it is reserved for God above
To sanctify to what far ends He will,
But which it only needs that we fulfill.

Robert Frost

Picture opposite
SPRING CARPET
Josef Muench

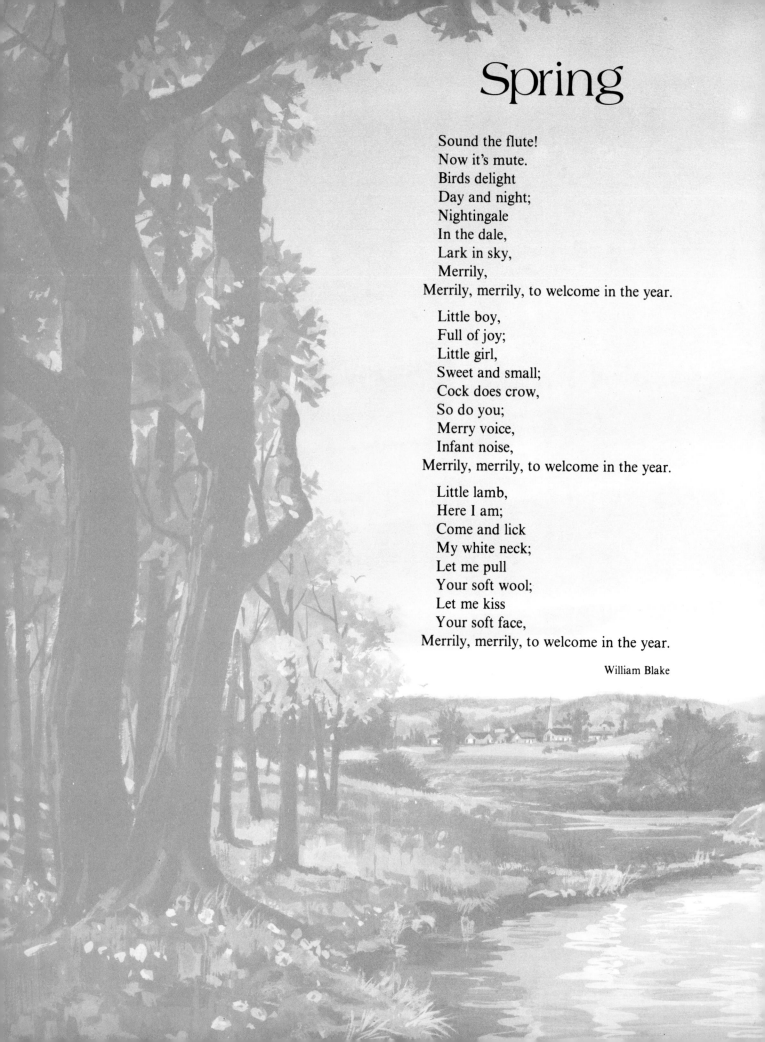

Spring

Sound the flute!
Now it's mute.
Birds delight
Day and night;
Nightingale
In the dale,
Lark in sky,
Merrily,
Merrily, merrily, to welcome in the year.

Little boy,
Full of joy;
Little girl,
Sweet and small;
Cock does crow,
So do you;
Merry voice,
Infant noise,
Merrily, merrily, to welcome in the year.

Little lamb,
Here I am;
Come and lick
My white neck;
Let me pull
Your soft wool;
Let me kiss
Your soft face,
Merrily, merrily, to welcome in the year.

William Blake

Written in March

The cock is crowing,
The stream is flowing,
The small birds twitter,
The lake doth glitter,
The green field sleeps in the sun;
The oldest and youngest
Are at work with the strongest;
The cattle are grazing,
Their heads never raising;
There are forty feeding like one!

Like an army defeated
The snow hath retreated,
And now doth fare ill
On the top of the bare hill;
The ploughboy is whooping—anon—anon.
There's joy in the mountains;
There's life in the fountains;
Small clouds are sailing,
Blue sky prevailing;
The rain is over and gone!

William Wordsworth

Spring Is Here

March comes in like a lamb — a petulant lamb perhaps — blustery, but with no real wind. Or it comes in like a fierce lion, with gusts and gales that rattle old tin roofs on sheds and barns, and makes farm windmills whirl and screak. If it comes in like a lamb, it will go out like a lion; or if it comes in like a lion, it will go out like a lamb. That's the theory, anyway.

In many places, there is yet time for some spring squalls of snow. And in these places, according to traditional weather prognosticators, even after the hardy forsythias have put forth their early yellow flowers, there will still be three more snows.

Merry kites of all colors, waving long white tails, soar and frolic on high. Spring freshets flow by the meadows, and alongside, the cowslips awaken. It is the springtime of the year. In woods and fields and along winding roads, Johnny-jump-ups jump up, and clover blossoms proclaim the season. In openings, throngs of elfin bluets are blooming, each with four tiny petals. If you like, you can call them innocence or Quaker-ladies.

Wisps of gossamer smoke still swirl up from red brick chimneys. Far above, flocks of wild geese in V-formations pass over the pale moon in the clear blue-gray starry sky as they travel northward to their summer home, and their faraway honking is faintly heard below. And green-headed wild mallard ducks swiftly wing their way north, too, toward their ancestral domains where they will build their nests in the

Overleaf
SCULPTURED GARDENS
Robert Cushman Hayes

marshes. Mourning doves fly up on whistling wings, and their throaty coos, that to us seem a little melancholy, are heard over the land. Already the pair in the old pine tree has a flimsy flat nest of twigs, stems, leaves, and moss with two white eggs. Under the eaves of the barn roof, the resident pair of barn owls has a set of pure white eggs.

If you know where there are some sassafras saplings growing, you can dig one up, wash the root clean, strip off the thick orangy rootbark, and have some old-fashioned "sassyfras tea." Sweet sap of sugar maple trees rises and flows from the taps, and from the sugar camp drift the delectable scents of maple syrup and maple sugar in the making.

Ground is broken in the vegetable garden, and the mellow fertile soil is smoothed with the garden rake. Hoes and trowels come out of storage, too, ready for a new growing season. Colorful seed packages make engrossing reading material. As you dig into the soil, a plump robin watches you with considerable interest and prepares to garner his own early harvest of tasty earthworms and grubs.

"Caw! Caw!" The cries of crows come from the distant woods. Over the field are heard the calls of the quails, "Bobwhite! Bob! Bobwhite!" Male red-winged blackbirds proudly display their brilliant scarlet and buff epaulets. Noisy flickers call loudly and with bobbing heads carve meticulous round nesting holes in trees, tossing wood chips to land where they may.

Crowds of crocuses in purple, yellow, and white appear jauntily in the new green grass. Grape hyacinths join the spectacle of springtime, and fragrant forget-me-nots, baby blue-eyes, bleeding hearts, sweet peas, and pinks arrive for extended visits.

From the gravelly banks down at the creek, excitable killdeers clamor, "Killdeer! Killdeer!" Industriously they search the pastures and fields for earthworms and insects.

Inconstant April arrives, with April showers and rainbows arching the sky. Jack-in-the-pulpit inhabits the woods. Dapper daffodils are yellow stars bestrewn across the ground. Birds' songs fill the air. Purple martins scout for homes. Hoptoads trill, tree frogs call, and the big bullfrog on the water-lily pad blows his throat into a bulging balloon and adds his bellowing bass notes to the chorus. Velvety gray catkins of pussy willows appear.

April becomes enchanted with the white and pink blossoms of apple, cherry, and plum trees sending forth their delicate sweet scents and buzzing with industrious honeybees. Spring is in the air! In the bough of the apple tree is tucked the nest of a pair of good neighbor robins, with a clutch of light greenish-blue eggs. Fragrant purple flowers of old-fashioned lilacs evoke nostalgic memories of springs past.

Richard L. Hawk

Blossoms in Springtime

So barren and bleak through the winter,
The victims of freezing or storm
Frail branches reach prayerfully upward
And wait for new buds to take form.

Each tenuous shoot pushes boldly,
Destroying the walls of its tomb;
New life shall explode from its prison
And suddenly burst into bloom.

The born-again blossoms in springtime —
Wild seeds sprouting up through the sod
Will display through magnificent beauty
The splendid creation of God.

Kay Long

An Easter Wish

Although we wish we could be there,
Bright flowers let you know we care.
Our bouquet comes to you to say,
"Have a very happy Easter Day."
Don't feel that you are all alone,
Our thoughts are there within your home.
So on this very special day,
Think not of us as miles away.
For in our hearts, we are there with you,
And you can be here with us, too.

Bart Gethmann

Easter Bunny's Secret

Old Jack Frost took his brushes,
   One crisp and chilly day,
And went to paint the countryside
   In colors bright and gay.

He touched his brush on every leaf,
   On every bush and tree,
And brightened up the whole wide world
   As far as eye could see.

The Easter Bunny followed him,
   And everywhere he found
Little bits of color that
   Had dribbled to the ground.

He scraped them up quite carefully
   That golden autumn day.
Oh, he was very busy
   In his funny bunny way!

And joy of joys, at evening time,
   Down in a quiet nook
He found the almost-empty pots
   By little Babbling Brook.

And now he had a secret
   He would tell on Easter Day.
The bunny smiled, and carefully
   He stored his paint away.

And then the winter settled down.
  The nights were dark and still.
The cold white snowflakes drifted
  In a heap on Bunny Hill.

But safe inside the bunny home,
  They waited for the spring
When crocus buds would open,
  And the Robin Redbreast sing.

And sometimes in the evening
  Just before they went to sleep,
They'd talk about the secret
  That it seemed they couldn't keep.

But something dreadful happened
  One awful winter day,
For naughty Frisky puppy
  Went into the woods to play.

He found the Easter Bunny's house;
  He scampered to and fro
And overturned the precious pots.
  The paint spilled in the snow!

*   *   *

Mother South Wind had a message
  That she whispered happily
To every tiny little flower,
  And every stately tree.

She gave it to the happy birds,
  And they began to sing
To pass along the precious word —
  Rejoice! for it is spring!

But in this world of brightness,
    In this world of cheer and song,
There was something out of order.
    There was something very wrong.

Mother South Wind went a-seeking,
    And to her dismay she found
Easter Bunny sobbing sadly
    With his nose pressed to the ground.

He told her all his troubles —
    His bunny tale of woe;
Then she hurried to your garden
    Where the brightest blossoms grow.

She told the pretty posies
    And the apple blossoms, too,
That the bunny needed colors —
    All the shades of every hue.

The lilacs offered purple,
    The shy Miss Violet, too;
The tulips and the hyacinths
    Gave yellow, red, and blue.

The apple blossoms offered pink,
    The cherries white and gold;
The daffodils gave all the orange
    His painting pots could hold.

Now his pots were full to bursting,
    And his heart was happy, too,
For he could tell his secret
    As he wished so much to do.

So if you think the flowers
    Aren't quite as bright a hue,
It's because they gave their colors
    To make Easter eggs for you!

Mrs. Roy L. Peifer

Dear Child:

Please to fancy, if you can, that you are reading a real letter from a real friend whom you have seen, and whose voice you can seem to yourself to hear, wishing you, as I do now with all my heart, a happy Easter.

Do you know that delicious, dreamy feeling, when one first wakes on a summer morning, with the twitter of birds in the air and the fresh breeze coming in at the open window — when, lying lazily with eyes half shut, one sees as in a dream green boughs waving or waters rippling in a golden light? It is a pleasure very near to sadness, bringing tears to one's eyes like a beautiful picture or poem. And is not that a mother's gentle hand that undraws your curtains, and a mother's sweet voice that summons you to rise? — to rise and forget, in the bright sunlight, the ugly dreams that frightened you so when all was dark — to rise and enjoy another happy day, first kneeling to thank that unseen Friend who sends you the beautiful sun?

Are these strange words from a writer of such tales as Alice? And is this a strange letter to find in a book of nonsense? It may be so. Some perhaps may blame one for thus mixing together things grave and gay; others may smile and think it odd that anyone should speak of solemn things at all, except in church and on Sunday; but I think — nay, I am sure — that some children will read this gently and lovingly, and in the spirit in which I have written it.

For I do not believe God means us thus to divide life into two halves, to wear a grave face on Sunday, and to think it out of place to even so much as mention Him on a weekday. Do you think He cares to see only kneeling

figures and to hear only tones of prayer; and that He does not also love to see the lambs leaping in the sunlight, and to hear the merry voices of the children as they roll among the hay? Surely their innocent laughter is as sweet in his ears as the grandest anthem that ever rolled up from the "dim, religious light" of some solemn cathedral.

And if I have written anything to add to those stories of innocent and healthy amusement that are laid up in books for the children I love so well, it is surely something I may hope to look back upon without shame and sorrow (as how much of life must then be recalled!) when my turn comes to walk through the valley of shadows.

This Easter sun will rise on you, dear child, feeling your "life in every limb" and eager to rush out into the fresh morning air, and many an Easter Day will come and go before it finds you feeble and gray-headed, creeping wearily out to bask once more in the sunlight; but it is good, even now, to think sometimes of that great morning when the "Sun of Righteousness shall arise with healing in his wings."

Surely your gladness need not be less for the thought that you will one day see a brighter dawn than this when livelier sights will meet your eyes than any waving trees or rippling waters, when angel hands shall undraw your curtains, and sweeter tones than ever loving mother breathed shall wake you to a new and glorious day, and when all the sadness and the sin that darkened this life on this little earth shall be forgotten like the dreams of a night that is past!

Lewis Carroll

Easter Chickens

When long-awaited spring has come
To greet us eagerly,
There's no place quite as busy as
The local hatchery.

The trays of eggs are turned each day
With utmost work and care
To nurture and protect the eggs
That will be hatching there.

Within the incubator's warmth,
The eggs progress each day,
And soon the chicks will flutter forth,
So soft in every way.

Small wonder, all the kids about
Wait so expectantly
For Easter chickens cuddly soft
Down at the hatchery.

Craig E. Sathoff

Barnyard Capers

Unusual happenings down at Farmer Brown's
Gave recourse for whispers and worried frowns.

Calls for a Sherlock to solve the matter
Soon filled the barnyard with ear-splitting clatter.

Hens from the hen house were raising a din,
Offering suggestions to poor mother hen.

Ducks were too busy to stop and look,
But they ordered the drake to go "case" the brook.

Clues soon appeared in the damp spring weather —
Five sets of prints and a small yellow feather.

Drake brought the good news. A flurry ensued.
Mother hen hurried to gather her brood.

The mystery was solved. The truth was out!
A chanticleer sounded his clarion shout.

Farmer Brown called it a seasonal thing.
Baby chicks got lost on their first spring fling.

Alice Leedy Mason

Back to Capistrano

I'll come back to Capistrano
With the swallows in the spring.
I shall hear you softly whisper
Love's sweet song and sweetly sing.
We shall meet inside the chapel
And the mission bells will ring.
I'll be back in Capistrano
With the swallows in the spring.

Ah, the year will go more swiftly
Knowing that you love me, too,
And the padre will be waiting
Just to welcome me and you.
And the birds will come as always
With their wedding tails and ties,
All atitter and atwitter
Neath the Capistrano skies.

We shall enter as a couple;
We shall leave as man and wife.
We shall pledge our troth in Heaven
That it last throughout our life.
We shall bless the birds that brought us
To this land so truly blessed,
All the way to Capistrano
In the bright and golden west.

I'll come back to Capistrano
With the swallows in the spring.
I shall hear you softly whisper
Love's sweet song and sweetly sing.
We shall meet inside the chapel
And the mission bells will ring.
I'll be back in Capistrano
With the swallows in the spring.

Minnie Klemme

The Iris

Ere yet the sun is high,
All blue the iris blossoms wave,
The colour of the sky.

Gasetsu

Crocuses

The sunrise tints the dew;
The yellow crocuses are out,
And I must pick a few.

Josa

Daffodils

In spite of cold and chills
That usher in the early spring
We have the daffodils.

Kikurio

Reprinted from A *Year of Japanese Epigrams* translated by William N. Porter (1911)
By permission of Oxford University Press, London

Picture opposite
CROCUSES
Alpha Photo Inc.

An Easter Carol

Spring bursts today,
    For Christ is risen and all the earth's at play.

    Flash forth, thou sun,
The rain is over and gone, its work is done.
    Winter is past,
Sweet Spring is come at last, is come at last.
    Bud, fig and vine,
Bud, olive, fat with fruit and oil and wine.
    Break forth this morn
In roses, thou but yesterday a thorn.
    Uplift thy head,
O pure white lily through the winter dead.
    Beside your dams
Leap and rejoice, you merry-making lambs.
    All herds and flocks
Rejoice, all beasts of thickets and of rocks.
    Sing, creatures, sing,
Angels and men and birds and everything.
    All notes of doves
Fill all our world; this is the time of loves.

Christina G. Rossetti

The Winter Is Past

My beloved spake, and said unto me, Rise up, my love, my fair one, and come away.

For, lo, the winter is past, the rain is over and gone;

The flowers appear on the earth; the time of the singing of birds is come, and the voice of the turtle is heard in our land;

The fig tree putteth forth her green figs, and the vines with the tender grapes give a good smell. Arise, my love, my fair one, and come away.

O my dove, that art in the clefts of the rock, in the secret places of the stairs, let me see thy countenance, let me hear thy voice; for sweet is thy voice, and thy countenance is comely.

Take us the foxes, the little foxes, that spoil the vines: for our vines have tender grapes.

My beloved is mine, and I am his: he feedeth among the lilies.

Until the day break, and the shadows flee away, turn, my beloved, and be thou like a roe or a young hart upon the mountains of Bether.

Song of Solomon 2:10-17

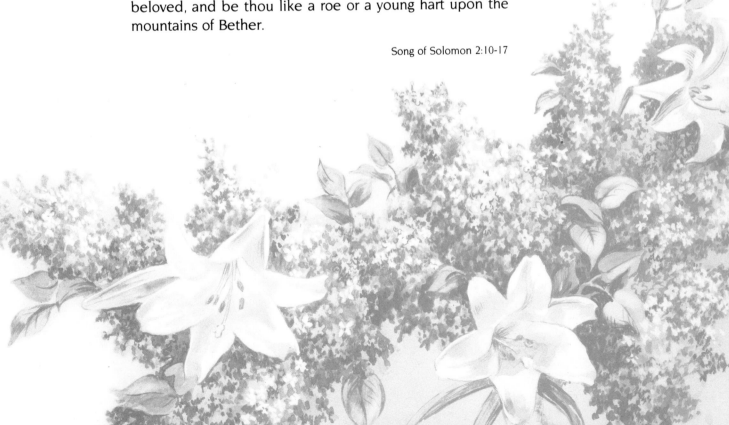

The Last Supper

Now the first day of the feast of unleavened bread the disciples came to Jesus, saying unto him, Where wilt thou that we prepare for thee to eat the passover? And he said, Go into the city to such a man, and say unto him, The Master saith, My time is at hand; I will keep the passover at thy house with my disciples. And the disciples did as Jesus had appointed them; and they made ready the passover. Now when the even was come, he sat down with the twelve. And as they did eat, he said, Verily I say unto you, that one of you shall betray me. And they were exceeding sorrowful, and began every one of them to say unto him, Lord, is it I? And he answered and said, He that dippeth his hand with me in the dish, the same shall betray me. The Son of man goeth as it is written of him: but woe unto that man by whom the Son of man is betrayed! it had been good for that man if he had not been born. Then Judas, which betrayed him, answered and said, Master, is it I? He said unto him, Thou hast said.

And as they were eating, Jesus took bread, and blessed it and brake it, and gave it to the disciples, and said, Take, eat; this is my body. And he took the cup, and gave thanks, and gave it to them, saying, Drink ye all of it; for this is my blood of the new testament, which is shed for many for the remission of sins. But I say unto you, I will not drink henceforth of this fruit of the vine, until that day when I drink it new with you in my Father's kingdom. And when they had sung an hymn, they went out into the mount of Olives. Then saith Jesus unto them, All ye shall be offended because of me this night: for it is written, I will smite the shepherd, and the sheep of the flock shall be scattered abroad. But after I am risen again, I will go before you into Galilee. Peter answered and said unto him, Though all men shall be offended because of thee, yet will I never be offended. Jesus said unto him, Verily I say unto thee, That this night, before the cock crow, thou shalt deny me thrice. Peter said unto him, Though I should die with thee, yet will I not deny thee. Likewise also said all the disciples.

Picture opposite
LAST SUPPER
Jerry Koser

Matthew 26:17-35

The portraits of Christ and the Apostles by the noted Spanish artist Jose Fuentes de Salamanca were first presented to Ideals readers in the 1977 Easter issue. Because so many of our readers responded enthusiastically to the artist's work, we feature it once again in this Easter tribute.

The character of each of the Apostles who followed Christ is subtly captured in these portraits, which many consider to be among the finest interpretations ever attempted.

We hope that you will find in them a continuing source of inspiration during this Easter season and throughout the years.

The Apostles of Jesus Christ

Jose Fuentes de Salamanca

Jose Fuentes works and lives in Spain. He has become one of the top-ranked artists in Spain, and his recognition and reputation continue to grow around the world.

In 1946 Fuentes was admitted into the Escuela de Artes y Oficios where he practiced drawing and completed his preliminary studies which would guide his brilliant career. In 1947 his first collective exposition was held in Santander where he received a special prize for his drawing of the Piedad.

In 1952 he exhibited numerous expositions where he was awarded economic assistance for his artistic studies by the Spanish Government's Ministry of Education; whereupon he entered the Real Academia de Bellas Artes of San Fernando in Madrid.

Jose Fuentes is versatile in almost every aspect and medium of the arts from fine oils to ink drawings.

The illustrations on the following pages were drawn by Jose Fuentes de Salamanca

Jesus Christ

Who hath believed our report? and to whom is the arm of the Lord revealed? For he shall grow up before him as a tender plant, and as a root out of a dry ground: he hath no form nor comeliness; and when we shall see him, there is no beauty that we should desire him. He is despised and rejected of men; a man of sorrows, and acquainted with grief: and we hid as it were our faces from him; he was despised, and we esteemed him not.

Surely he hath borne our griefs, and carried our sorrows: yet we did esteem him stricken, smitten of God, and afflicted. But he was wounded for our transgressions, he was bruised for our iniquities: the chastisement of our peace was upon him; and with his stripes we are healed. All we like sheep have gone astray; we have turned every one to his own way; and the Lord hath laid on him the iniquity of us all. He was oppressed, and he was afflicted, yet he opened not his mouth: he is brought as a lamb to the slaughter, and as a sheep before her shearers is dumb, so he openeth not his mouth. He was taken from prison and from judgment: and who shall declare his generation? for he was cut off out of the land of the living: for the transgression of my people was he stricken. And he made his grave with the wicked, and with the rich in his death; because he had done no violence, neither was any deceit in his mouth.

Yet it pleased the Lord to bruise him; he hath put him to grief: when thou shalt make his soul an offering for sin, he shall see his seed, he shall prolong his days, and the pleasure of the Lord shall prosper in his hand. He shall see of the travail of his soul, and shall be satisfied: by his knowledge shall my righteous servant justify many; for he shall bear their iniquities. Therefore will I divide him a portion with the great, and he shall divide the spoil with the strong; because he hath poured out his soul unto death: and he was numbered with the transgressors; and he bare the sin of many, and made intercession for the transgressors.

Isaiah 53

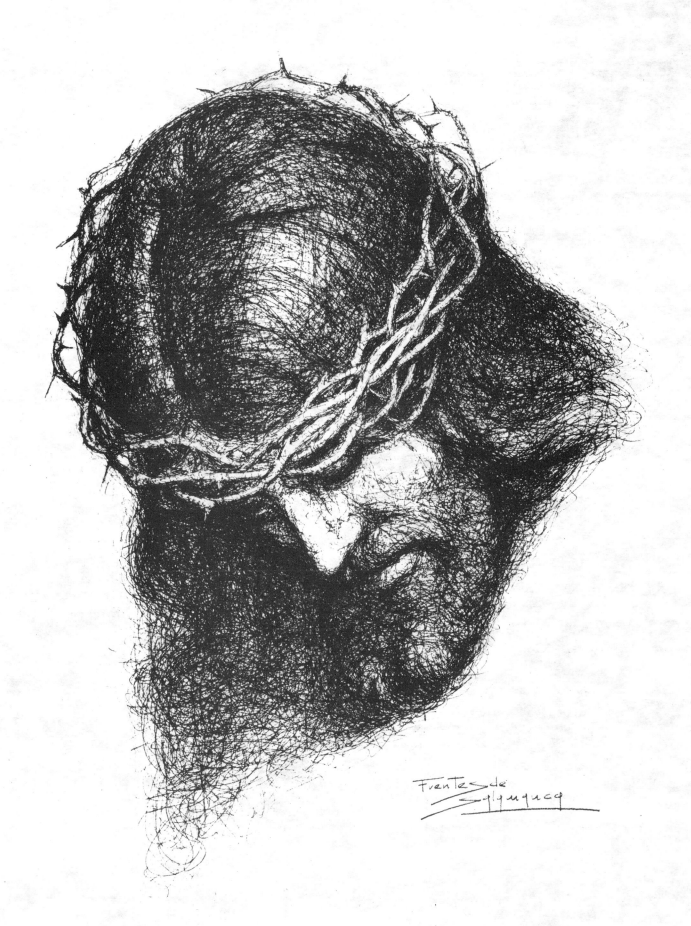

And when it was day, he called unto him his disciples: and of them he chose twelve, whom also he named apostles; Simon (whom he also named Peter,) and Andrew his brother, James and John, Philip and Bartholomew, Matthew and Thomas, James the son of Alpheus, and Simon called Zelotes, and Judas the brother of James, and Judas Iscariot, which also was the traitor.

Luke 6:13-16

Peter

There was Peter, a fisherman from the shores of Lake Genesareth. Peter was the most frequent spokesman of the Apostolic band, traveling to Antioch and Rome, healing the sick.

Andrew

Another fisherman was Andrew from Capernaum, the first disciple named in John's Gospel. Andrew was one of the inner circle, preaching around the Black Sea in Cappadocia, Russia, Byzantium, Macedonia, and Thessaly. He is believed to have died in Patras, Greece.

John

The beloved disciple was John, the only one remaining faithful to the Master during his passion. John's ministry took him all through Asia Minor. Eventually exiled in Patmos, he is reputed to have been buried in Ephesus.

James

The first disciple to suffer martyrdom was John's brother James the Greater. He became the first apostle of Spain, and his emblem is the pilgrim's staff. James was put to death by the sword at the order of Herod Agrippa.

Philip

Fifth among the twelve was Philip, a native of Bethsaida. He was shy, naive, and sober-minded. He was present at the miracle of the loaves and fishes. Philip's apostolate took him to Scythia where he eventually died in Hieropolis.

Bartholomew

It was Philip who introduced Bartholomew to Christ. His missionary labors brought him to India, Mesopotamia, and Parthia.

Matthew

The seventh named was Matthew or "Jehovah's Gift." A Galilean by birth, he was a tax gatherer by trade. Originally known as Levi, Matthew was present at the resurrection and ascension, and is symbolized as a winged man.

Thomas

Working with Matthew was Thomas, the first disciple to acknowledge Christ's divinity. It was Thomas who questioned the Resurrection until he was shown the wounds in his Master's hands and side.

James the Less

Called to the apostolate during the second year of Christ's ministry was James the Less. His father's name was Alpheus, and his mother was one of the Marys who went to Jesus' tomb on Easter morning.

Jude

The brother of James the Less was Jude, who came from the party of the zealots. A patron of desperate causes, Jude's missionary work took him to Palestine, Syria, Mesopotamia, and eventually to his martyrdom in Persia.

Simon

Martyred along with Saint Jude was the "Cana-
nean" Simon, who possessed a zeal for the Jewish
law. He preached along the Black Sea and in
Egypt and North Africa. He is reputed to have
died in Iberia although there is no record of his
tomb.

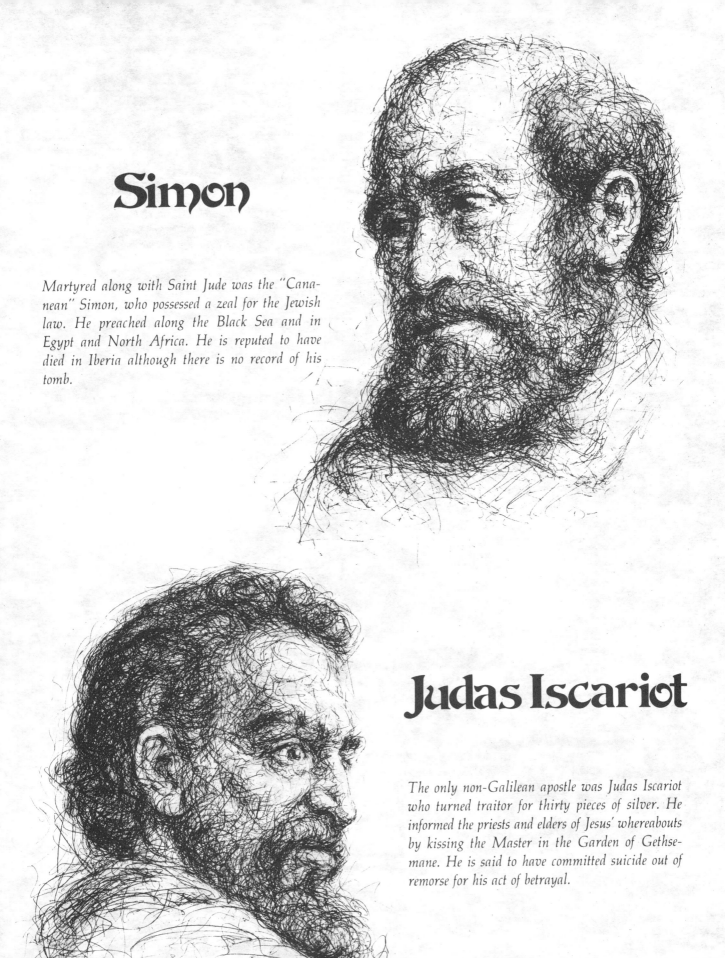

Judas Iscariot

The only non-Galilean apostle was Judas Iscariot
who turned traitor for thirty pieces of silver. He
informed the priests and elders of Jesus' whereabouts
by kissing the Master in the Garden of Gethse-
mane. He is said to have committed suicide out of
remorse for his act of betrayal.

The Crucifixion

And they bring him unto the place Golgotha, which is, being interpreted,
The place of a skull. And they gave him to drink wine mingled with
myrrh: but he received it not. And when they had crucified him, they
parted his garments, casting lots upon them, what every man should take.
And it was the third hour, and they crucified him. And the superscrip-
tion of his accusation was written over, THE KING OF THE JEWS.

Mark 15:22-26

The Resurrection

In the end of the sabbath, as it began to dawn toward the first day of the week, came Mary Magdalene and the other Mary to see the sepulchre. And, behold, there was a great earthquake: for the angel of the Lord descended from heaven, and came and rolled back the stone from the door, and sat upon it. His countenance was like lightning, and his raiment white as snow: and for fear of him the keepers did shake, and became as dead men. And the angel answered and said unto the women, Fear not ye: for I know that ye seek Jesus, which was crucified. He is not here: for he is risen, as he said. Come, see the place where the Lord lay. And go quickly, and tell his disciples that he is risen from the dead; and, behold, he goeth before you into Galilee; there shall ye see him: lo, I have told you. And they departed quickly from the sepulchre with fear and great joy; and did run to bring his disciples word.

Matthew 28:1-8

Easter Hymn

Christ the Lord is risen today,
Sons of men and angels say;
Raise your joys and triumphs high,
Sing, ye heavens, and earth reply.

Love's redeeming work is done,
Fought the fight, the battle won;
Lo! our Sun's eclipse is o'er;
Lo! He sets in blood no more.

Vain the stone, the watch, the seal;
Christ hath burst the gates of hell!
Death in vain forbids his rise;
Christ hath opened Paradise!

Lives again our glorious King;
Where, O Death, is now thy sting?
Once He died, our souls to save;
Where thy victory, O Grave?

Charles Wesley

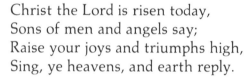

Picture opposite
TRUMPETS AND LILIES
H. Armstrong Roberts

William Arnette Wofford

William Arnette Wofford was a prolific, successful writer of both prose and poetry covering a wide range of themes and interests. *Ideals* initially published a poem by Mr. Wofford in 1957; since then his verses have appeared often in *Ideals* and have continued to bring pleasure to many readers. A resident of South Carolina during his lifetime, William Wofford was an elementary school teacher.

I Wish

I wish I could have seen His face
All radiant that Easter morn;
A great light shining on His brow
That had been pierced by many a thorn.

I wish I could have seen His smile,
After the darkness and the gloom,
When Mary kissed His garment's hem
In wonder by the open tomb.

I wish I could have heard Him speak
There in the April garden when
He walked among the lilies and
Proclaimed eternal life for men.

But wishing is in vain, I know,
So I must be content to see
The miracle recurring in
Each blossomed bud and leaf and tree.

There is a warm assurance, too,
That of His love I am a part
And that His resurrection lives
Forever in my heart.

Easter Dawn

It was yet dark when Mary reached
The shadowed garden, chill with gloom,
Coming with loved ones pierced with grief
To bring the spices to the tomb.

It was yet dark; she scarce could see
The sepulcher before her there,
And when she found the great stone moved,
Her sorrow seemed too great to bear.

The stone that had imprisoned Him
For three long days was rolled away!
It was yet dark, but even so,
A faint light showed the breaking day!

With darkness of the night dispelled,
The woman heard words strangely sweet;
She turned and saw her Master near
And fell there sobbing at his feet.

Oh, wondrous joy beyond belief
For Mary then, with darkness gone,
To see upon the garden path
The newly risen Lord at dawn!

The Last Supper

Now when the eventide was come
With shadows deepening into gloom,
Came Jesus with the twelve and sat
At supper in the upper room.

A solemn hush fell over them,
And in the soft gold candlelight,
His heart was heavy, for He knew
His hour was near at hand that night.

And while they ate, He reverently
Began to bless and break the bread,
"This is my body given for you;
Take ye and eat," the Master said.

He took the cup, and giving thanks
He gave it to them lovingly.
"This is my blood, drink ye of it;
Do this in memory of me."

They would remember all their lives
The poignant beauty in his face,
And treasure, too, the blessed words
He spoke there in that quiet place.

I Went in Search of Spring

I went in search of spring today;
So tired was I of winter's cold;
Eager was I to see again
A blossomed daffodil's bright gold.

And then upon a windswept hill,
Beneath March trees still bare, I found
A field of blowing daffodils
That seemed to stretch for miles around.

A hillside turned to glimmering gold —
Oh, loveliness too great to bear!
Then suddenly I heard the first
Red robin's song upon the air.

Along the road, a wild plum tree
Had blossomed white as drifted snow;
And on the pussy willow bush,
I saw the silky catkins glow.

When I turned homeward, I was glad,
For I had heard the first red robin sing
And had my fill of daffodils —
The first bright harbingers of spring.

These Are the Things

These are the things that tell me now
Spring's lovely miracle has come:
The flash of redbirds on the wing,
White blossoms of the roadside plum,

The farmer plowing in the field,
The pussy willow's soft gray sheen,
The bright parade of hyacinths,
And willow streamers turning green,

Buds swelling on the lilac bush,
The golden flame of daffodils.
Blowing down the keen March wind,
And maples glowing on the hills.

Always these are the first to show
That winter has outlived his day
And that the road is clear at last
For spring's returning down the way.

Daffodils in the Rain

Nothing I have ever seen
Is lovelier than silver rain
Falling on gold daffodils
In bloom along my garden lane.

Overnight they have appeared,
As if by magic, from the ground.
Grateful for their first rain bath,
They revel in its friendly sound.

Golden beauty blinding me
Along the path and garden wall,
Winter's bondage now has ceased
With spring's enchanting first sweet call.

A Tribute to Frances Hook

Ideals offers this tribute to the memory of Frances Hook, one of our best-loved illustrators of children. Frances Hook died July 23, 1983, at the age of seventy in her hometown of Boothbay Harbor, Maine.

She was born near Pittsburgh and attended the Pennsylvania Museum School of Art where she studied under the noted illustrator Harry Pitz. Even at that time, her subject matter and style were evident; she featured children in soft pastel colors. After graduation, Frances married artist Richard Hook and then began her career as a freelance artist.

Her first assignment, a two-page ad for General Electric, appeared in the *Saturday Evening Post*. She later designed ads for Steinway Pianos, General Mills, and Hallmark Cards. She gained public recognition in the late 1950s and early 1960s when she created the now-famous illustrations for Northern Tissue.

Frances often worked with her husband on an illustration; she would do the women and children while Richard drew the men.

Original artwork by Frances Hook is on permanent exhibit at The Old School in Mishicot, Wisconsin. The Frances Hook Gallery was dedicated on Father's Day weekend, 1982.

Painting opposite
EASTER EGG HUNT
Frances Hook

Readers' Reflections

April Foolishness

First she said she thought she could;
Then she said she couldn't;
Then she said she guessed she would;
Then she said she wouldn't.
First she smiled a teardrop;
Then she frowned a shower,
Turned the sky from gray to blue
And back within the hour.

Winsome as a sweetheart,
Demanding as a shrew,
Wouldn't say exactly
What she planned to do;
Somber as December,
Radiant as June,
Faithful Spring will pay the piper —
Faithless April calls the tune.

Julia Collins Ardayne

Easter Fulfillment

It's sunup, Easter morning,
And at the break of day,
Old Mr. Hare is wide awake
And far upon his way.
He carries eggs to children
Still sleeping in their beds,
His baskets filled with rainbows
Of blues and golds and reds.

It's sundown, Easter evening,
And who is this we see
Tucked snugly in his cozy hutch
And dreaming happily?
It is the selfsame Mr. Hare
Whose yearly work is done,
And he has earned a welcome rest
For spreading Easter fun.

Marguerite Gode

Easter Joys

As bright as Easter's gayest flowers
Are these wishes that I send,
For the season's richest joys
That never, never end!

Pearl McKinney

Editor's Note: In future issues of Ideals we hope to dedicate several pages to submissions from our readers. We will feature poetry, short anecdotes, and humorous reflections on life. Every submission received will be considered for publication.

Baby Chick

As yellow as butter,
Like a soft cotton ball,
Is the new little chick
With its cheep-cheeping call.

Its sparkly black eyes
Are as round as can be
As I hold it so gently
And then set it free

To run all about
On its little orange feet,
Pecking at grain bits
I give it to eat.

Dear little chicken,
You're one of the things
I'm glad that the coming
Of Easter time brings!

Virginia Blanck Moore

First Season

Spring is a crocus
Blooming too soon,
A ringing at dawning,
A first-quarter moon,
A flurry of snow
That lasts half an hour,
A warming of sun,
A sudden strong shower,
A waking and quaking
Of reeds in the pond,
A loud laughing stream
In the meadow beyond.
Spring is a pushing,
A trembling, a groping,
A moping, a yawning,
A dawning, a hoping.

Meta Pfeiffer

Spring Ritual

Today I saw an act of faith;
A man was on his knees,
Not in a pew, but by a fence,
Planting apple trees.

Sudie Stuart Hager

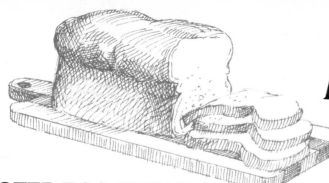

Easter Breads

EASTER EGG BREAD

Makes 2.

12 uncooked eggs
    Egg coloring
½ cup milk, scalded
½ cup sugar
 1 teaspoon salt
½ cup butter
    Grated peel of 2
    lemons

 2 packages dry yeast
½ cup warm water
 2 eggs, slightly beaten
4½ cups flour
 1 egg, beaten
    Tiny decorating
    candies

Wash eggs; tint shells with egg coloring and set aside. To the scalded milk, add sugar, salt, butter, and lemon peel; cool to lukewarm. Dissolve yeast in warm water; add to milk mixture with the 2 eggs and 2½ cups flour. Beat until smooth. Stir in enough remaining flour, a little at a time, to form a dough that is easy to handle. Place on a lightly floured board and knead until smooth and elastic, 5 to 8 minutes. Place in a lightly greased bowl, turning dough once to grease the top. Cover and let rise in a warm place until doubled in bulk. Punch down; let rise again. Divide dough into 4 parts; form each part into a 36-inch rope. On a greased baking sheet, shape 2 ropes into a loosely braided ring, leaving spaces for 6 eggs. Repeat with the other 2 ropes of dough for the second ring. Insert the colored eggs in each ring. Cover and let rise until doubled in bulk. Brush evenly with beaten egg. Sprinkle with decorating candies. Bake in a preheated 375° oven 20 minutes or until lightly browned. Serve warm.

FROSTED EASTER ROLLS

Thaw a 1-pound loaf of frozen cinnamon *or* raisin bread dough. Allow to rise until doubled in bulk. Break off pieces of dough; roll each piece into the shape of an egg. Place "eggs" in a lightly greased pie plate. Bake in a preheated 350° oven about 25 minutes or until lightly browned. Cool on a wire rack. When cool, decorate "eggs" with colored frostings.

KULICH
(Russian Easter Cake)

Makes 2.

 2 46-ounce juice cans
1½ cups milk, scalded
    and cooled
5½ to 6 cups flour
 1 package dry yeast
¼ cup warm water
 4 egg yolks
⅔ cup sugar
¼ cup lemon-flavored
    instant tea
 1 teaspoon water

 1 cup butter **or**
    margarine, melted
⅔ cup chopped
    blanched almonds
⅓ cup grated lemon
    peel
¼ teaspoon salt
    Pinch saffron
⅓ cup seedless golden
    raisins
    White Lemon Glaze

Line the juice cans with greased brown paper; set aside. In a large bowl, combine cooled milk and 4 cups flour. Dissolve yeast in water; stir into the flour mixture. Cover and let rise in a warm place until doubled in bulk. In a small bowl, beat egg yolks with sugar until light and thick; blend in tea and 1 teaspoon water; stir into dough. Add butter and blend well. Stir in nuts, lemon peel, salt, saffron, and raisins. Gradually stir in enough flour to make the dough firm enough to handle; place on a floured board and knead until smooth and elastic, working in additional flour as needed. Divide the dough in half and place in the prepared juice cans. Cover and let rise in a warm place until doubled in bulk. Bake in a preheated 375° oven about 1¼ hours or until golden brown. Allow to cool 5 minutes. Remove loaves from containers; cool on a wire rack. When cool, stand loaves upright and spread tops with White Lemon Glaze, allowing the glaze to drizzle down the sides.

White Lemon Glaze

½ cup confectioners' sugar
 2 teaspoons hot water
 1 teaspoon lemon juice

In a small bowl, combine confectioners' sugar, water, and lemon juice; blend well.

Picture opposite
EASTER BREADS
Jerry Koser

Easter Customs Around the World

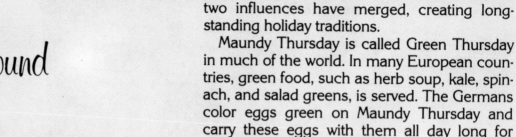

Many customs connected with the Easter season come from pagan festivals of spring, while others stem from the Passover celebration. In many countries around the world, the two influences have merged, creating long-standing holiday traditions.

Maundy Thursday is called Green Thursday in much of the world. In many European countries, green food, such as herb soup, kale, spinach, and salad greens, is served. The Germans color eggs green on Maundy Thursday and carry these eggs with them all day long for good luck.

The giving of alms has come to be associated with Maundy Thursday. Queen Elizabeth I of England is rumored to have washed the feet of a poor person, using a basin of water filled with sweet-smelling herbs, spices, and flowers. In England today, the custom is somewhat updated as the queen gives money to the poor every Holy Thursday.

Foot washing on that day is still an important custom in other countries, however. The pope washes the feet of thirteen of his associates at Saint Peter's Cathedral in Rome. Twelve of them symbolize the apostles. The thirteenth represents the angel who reportedly appeared in the sixth century at the table of Gregory the Great when he was carrying out the foot-washing tradition. In Spain, the archbishop washes the feet of thirteen poor elderly people who are then wined and dined by religious officials.

Maundy Thursday is also associated with cleansing in other folk traditions. In Slavic countries, men in rural districts leave their homes at midnight on Maundy Thursday and go to a nearby river or stream to wash themselves.

Good Friday has also generated its share of customs and superstitions. Generations ago in Europe, people didn't wash clothes on Good Friday because they believed the laundry would be stained with bloodlike spots. Blacksmiths wouldn't nail horseshoes that day because they associated the nails with those driven through Christ's hands to the cross. Gypsies would not wash their hands on Good Friday because they remembered Pontius Pilate's hand-washing ritual.

Good Friday was considered a good omen, however, in some countries. It was supposed to be a lucky day for farmers — a good day to plant parsley, peas, beans, and fruit trees. If it rained on that day, the rain was supposed to have remarkable curative powers, especially for persons with eye trouble — if they were lucky enough to be able to catch and keep some of the rainwater. People who died on Good Friday were envied; they were said to have joined the Good Thief in a speedy entry to Heaven.

In England, eating hot cross buns was supposed to ward off bad luck. People who were concerned about keeping rats out of their corn-fields, or preventing fires and shipwrecks, tried to protect themselves from such catastrophes by eating the buns. Legend says hot cross buns were first made in 1361 at Saint Alban's Abbey when a monk baked them to give to the poor.

Thousands of worshipers make pilgrimages to Rome during Holy Week for services at Saint Peter's.

On Easter Eve in Romania, churchgoers carry lighted candles home from midnight mass. When they arrive home, the young people gaze into mirrors by candlelight to try to see into the future.

Easter Sunday is traditionally a time for dressing up in new spring fashions. An old Easter rhyme sums it up, "At Easter let your clothes be new, or else be sure you will it rue."

Many special foods have become associated with Easter; among them are Easter breads, hot cross buns, and decorated pastries. Pork and lamb are the two main meats served for Easter dinner around the world. In this country, ham is traditional, stemming from the English custom established in the days of William the Conqueror. The pig was a symbol of good luck and prosperity in many lands, and thus was appropriate for representing the bounty of Easter. Lamb is still the favored Easter meat in many parts of eastern Europe, probably because of its religious connotations.

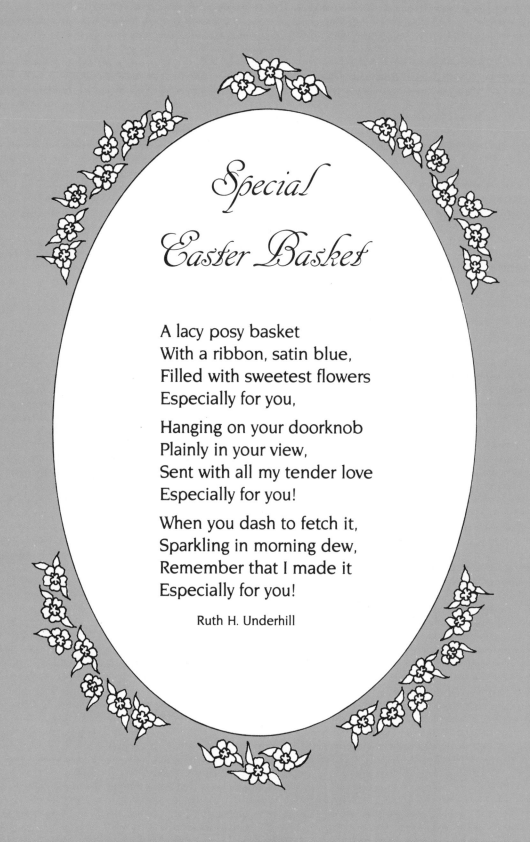

Special
Easter Basket

A lacy posy basket
With a ribbon, satin blue,
Filled with sweetest flowers
Especially for you,

Hanging on your doorknob
Plainly in your view,
Sent with all my tender love
Especially for you!

When you dash to fetch it,
Sparkling in morning dew,
Remember that I made it
Especially for you!

Ruth H. Underhill

Picture opposite
EASTER GREETING
Fred Sieb

The Easter Parade

A composer who cannot read music and who plays the piano only in the key of F-sharp has become one of the most popular American songwriters of the twentieth century. Irving Berlin has published about fifteen hundred songs, many of them familiar throughout the world today. Some of his best-known songs include "Alexander's Ragtime Band," "White Christmas," and "Easter Parade."

In 1948, Metro-Goldwyn-Mayer began production of *Easter Parade*, the musical featuring the songs of Irving Berlin. The movie co-starred Fred Astaire and Judy Garland. Gene Kelly had actually contracted for the lead role, but he broke an ankle while playing touch football with some children in his backyard. Fred Astaire was his replacement. Astaire had been in semiretirement for several years, devoting his time to establishing dance studios and breeding race horses. But he was persuaded to return to the screen, and *Easter Parade* turned out to be one of his best performances and one of the most successful musicals of the decade.

Forty-eight-year-old Astaire played the part of a nimble-footed 1912 vaudeville dancer who is rejected by his ambitious dancing partner. He decides to make a carbon copy of his former partner from the very first girl he meets. That girl turns out to be Judy Garland who plays a chorus girl with greater aspirations for fame and fortune. As they begin to work together, she falls in love with him, but he has time for nothing but his work. She chides him for being "nothing but a pair of dancing shoes." He soon discovers her charms as well as her talents and begins to reciprocate her love.

The musical is rich with Berlin classics performed by Astaire and Garland. Movie audiences were treated to the old favorites, "When That Midnight Choo-Choo Leaves for Alabam," "The Girl on the Magazine Cover," and, of course, "Easter Parade." The old songs blended well with the new which included "A Feller with an Umbrella," "Steppin' Out with My Baby," and the classic tramp song of all time, "A Couple of Swells."

Photo opposite
EASTER PARADE
The Bettmann Archive, Inc.

Springtime's Charm

All gardens work great wonders
At this time every year,
Producing flowers and shrubbery
As summertime draws near.

Lilac bushes have put on
Their very finest gown
In royal shades of purple
Befitting any crown.

Tulips in their turbans gay
Of scarlet, pink, and green
Add vivid color against the grass
Which takes on added sheen.

Trees leaf out and birds return
And days are bright and fair,
For earth puts out a welcome sign
When spring is in the air.

Carice Williams

Bicycles

With the coming of the first warm, balmy days of spring, the bicyclist performs his annual ritual. He hauls his bicycle out of winter storage, freeing it at last from the confines of basement or garage. Hasty with anticipation, he de-cobwebs it, gives it a quick tune-up, and adds air to the winter-deflated tires. He hops aboard then, ready for the first glorious ride of the year. The bicycle is one of the sure signs of spring's arrival. But it wasn't always so! Imagine life, and spring, before bicycles.

No one knows exactly when the bicycle was invented. The earliest known picture of something resembling a bicycle is dated 1642 and appears in a stained glass window in a church in Stokes Pages, England. It is unclear whether the artist referred to an actual machine for his artistic inspiration, or whether he relied entirely on his imagination. Bicycle-like machines were in existence before 1800. About 1790, a Frenchman is reported to have invented a "walk-along." The rider propelled the two-wheeled vehicle by sitting on a padded saddle and pushing the ground, crab-like, with his feet. Unfortunately, the machine could not be easily steered. Nevertheless, several such devices were in use by the late 1700s. They were quite popular with the French upper classes.

The basic design was improved in both France and Germany around 1818. This improved vehicle could be steered. The Draisienne was named after Baron Karl von Drais of Sauerbrun who used the machine extensively in his travels, since he was not fond of horses. Shortly thereafter, Dennis Johnson of London began manufacturing the Draisienne. Eventually, two distinct versions were made, one for men and one for women. The men's style included a horizontal bar, and the ladies' did not, similar to the distinction still made today. Because leisure was a luxury only the wealthy could afford, the machines came to be known, rather disparagingly, as dandy horses or hobbyhorses.

The next big development in the bicycle came in 1840 when Kirkpatrick Macmillan, a Scottish blacksmith, fit pedals to the bicycle.

Indeed, most historians credit Macmillan with inventing the bicycle. He took a dandy horse, added cranks, pedals, and driving rods to it, and built a comfortable seat, elaborate armrests, and handlebars. Macmillan rode the machine everywhere for many years. He has the dubious distinction of being the first bicyclist to have been brought before a magistrate. He apparently hit a pedestrian and was fined for "furious driving."

In 1870, the "penny-farthing," also called the "high-wheeler" or "ordinary," emerged in England. The front wheel of these early bicycles tended to get bigger and bigger, supposedly to attain more speed. Front wheels of fifty inches diameter became common, with rear wheels of about seventeen inches. The penny-farthing was popular in many countries for a decade or more, although it had basic design faults. It was difficult to mount and dismount, and had a tendency to tip over headfirst when it bumped into an obstacle.

After several more stages, an Englishman named J. K. Starley developed his "Rover," an early prototype of the bicycle today. In 1888, the air-filled tire was invented. By the 1890s, the bicycle had matured. The typical design, called a safety bicycle, looked much like the bicycle of today, with two twenty-eight-inch wheels, a chain drive, and air-filled tires.

Photo opposite
BICYCLING
The Bettmann Archive, Inc.

Silent Picture Shows

Thomas Alva Edison set the movie industry in motion. The inventor himself was not all that impressed with the concept of motion pictures; he figured the novelty would quickly wear off. How wrong he was!

The first "moving" pictures in 1889 were peep shows viewed through Edison's Kinetoscope. A length of film revolved on spools inside a cabinet. When a coin was dropped into a slot, an electric light shone on the film. The viewer watched the film through a peephole just big enough for the human eye. The films were about fifty feet in length and ran for less than a minute. Some early Edison films featured a dog with a bone, a baby being bathed, dances, and vaudeville scenes.

By 1908, the American public had become fascinated with the idea of movies, and nickelodeons were being built all over the country. Although these early motion picture theaters lacked the luxuries of today's plush theaters in mall settings, the magic of Hollywood was perhaps even more alive in those early days than it is now because of its novelty. And although sound had not been invented, moviegoers used their imaginations to supply the dialogue to the events taking place before them on the screen. The era of the silent movie had begun.

It didn't take producers long to discover which genres worked well in silent films. Comedy became popular early in the industry's development. The *Keystone Kops* series was the most successful of the early comedy series. The *Keystone Kops* featured fast-paced, slapstick humor and often violent action; typical escapades included the pie in the face, the wild car chase scene, and wild animals on the loose. Actor/producer Mack Sennett came to Los Angeles in 1912 to work for the Keystone Company. Sennett gave many comedians their start in films, including Charlie Chaplin and Buster Keaton.

Charles Spencer Chaplin became the most recognized film figure in the world during the era of the silent movie. Chaplin added depth of character and plot structure to the developing art form, rather than relying on simple gags and gimmicks for laughs. His tramp character, for which he became famous, first appeared in *Kid Auto Races at Venice* (1914). The tramp's costume was appealing and immediately identifiable — the too-big shoes and pants, the formal vest, and the too-small coat. The derby hat, which he doffed to all he met, contrasted with his funny moustache, and it, too, became a trademark of the little tramp's character. Some of Chaplin's most famous movies included *The Kid* (1920), *The Gold Rush* (1925), and *City Lights* (1931).

Chaplin's biggest rival was Buster Keaton who began in films in 1917. Keaton capitalized on dream sequences and trick photography to enhance his art. In two of his best films, *The Navigator* (1924) and *The General* (1926), Keaton dealt with the same theme — the individual pitting his will against an inanimate object. It was the theme that worked the best for him, and he made the most of it.

Stan Laurel and Oliver Hardy are probably the most memorable team in the history of silent films. Actually, they entered the industry separately; it wasn't until 1927 that they began to work as a team. Tall, thin Laurel was the perfect foil for fat and pompous Hardy. Incompetence ruled their world and endeared them to their audiences. In *The Music Box* (1932), the two struggle valiantly to get a piano up a flight of stairs half a mountain high, only to succeed in destroying everything in their path and the piano itself. Two of the best-known Laurel and Hardy films, *Our Relations* and *Way Out West,* were produced after the advent of sound. The two made the transition to sound more effectively than either Chaplin or Keaton.

By 1929 the silent-film era was nearing its end. The technology for "talkies" had been developed, and silent-screen stars were frantically studying voice and diction in an attempt to make the transition. The majority of theaters throughout the country had been wired for sound. Silent pictures were about to become film history.

Overleaf
WHITE TULIPS
Fred Sieb

Overleaf
COLORADO SPRINGTIME
Josef Muench

Gladys Taber's
April

Early morning is like a pink pearl now that April's here. The first lilacs are budding over the white picket fence in the Quiet Garden; crocus, daffodils, white and purple grape hyacinths repeat the magic of spring. Surely never was spring so wonderful, such a miracle! For it seems only yesterday that drifts piled high in the little garden as I made my mittened and booted way to the kennel. My heart remembers this with surprise as I examine the delicate papery bud tips on my favorite King Alfred white daffodils.

The King Alfred has a silvery cup with a faint glow in the heart almost like old polished ivory. I really wonder why it was named King Alfred — not that it isn't a royal flower but that it does not look masculine. It reminds me of a tall and gentle medieval princess robed in ivory velvet.

The early flowers have a special beauty — I always shake with excitement when I find the first clump of snowdrops, fragile, pearl-pure, bending their heads lightly toward the icy dark ground. Crocus make rainbow patches all over the yard; scilla looks like bits of the sky snipped out and scattered down.

George plows around the nineteenth of the month. I often think that when we bought the farm, we had no idea that George was going to go with it, so to speak. In fact, we wished there was no farm across the road but rather one of those breathtaking views of valley and blue mountains. George finds time to run a full-going farm with a dairy herd, and yet to come every morning to help feed dogs, run the furnace, chop firewood, lug heavy cartons. If the car doesn't start, George gets it going. If my bed falls to pieces in the night, he puts new slats in, wires it up again.

He fixes faucets, repairs the wall can opener. If the dogs get out of the gate, he comes running from the barn to scoop them up. If he is cutting hay in his upper field and we get in trouble, we lean on the picket fence and yell.

He is my idea of a true Yankee, ingenious beyond measure, steadfast, sound. And never a day so dark but that George comes in with the sunniest smile and an air of great cheer. We lean on him; we have leaned on him shamelessly since he was a teenager rolling down the road on his old hay wagon.

Actually George's father fled from Lithuania to escape being drafted into the army long years ago, and he sent back for his bride as soon has he was established in the new country.

The children grew up speaking Lithuanian at home, and Connecticut at school. There wasn't much school either as the three boys went to work on the farm just as soon as possible.

Frank, the oldest boy, helped us in the beginning, and when he married and moved away, Willie took over. Willie wanted more school; he went to the nearest vocational school and got through with flying flags, even though he often had to miss time during haying or butchering or rebuilding barns. He used to come over to study in the evening and talk about his dreams. When he went in the navy, I don't know who cried harder, his mother or me. But at his wedding, the family said I cried harder than anybody. I loved his bride too. A mechanical genius, Willie did not want to farm, so when he came home, he went in the tool-shop in Waterbury, and we sliced off a piece of our land for his house to be built on.

From then on, George swung into place as our help and comfort. And when he married, we sliced a little more off for his house. Such a snug cozy feeling to have them right down the road beyond the old apple orchard.

When George comes to plow, we stop everything and rush to watch. George loves it too; he is laughing as he wheels the great tractor around, and manages to skip the asparagus bed by the measure of a very thin dime. As the great shining blades fold the dark earth over, the long rich furrows roll out. And I think a man who plows rides the world. You can feel the great old Mother Earth being released from winter rigidity, and giving again her richness to mankind. You feel this mystery of growth which so far man has not destroyed. Plant well, says the soil, and I will nourish you once again.

From STILLMEADOW DAYBOOK. Copyright 1955 by Gladys Taber. Copyright renewed 1983 by Constance Taber Colby.

Spring in Carolina

Spring, with that nameless pathos in the air
Which dwells with all things fair,
Spring, with her golden suns and silver rain,
Is with us once again.

Out in the lonely woods the jasmine burns
Its fragrant lamps, and turns
Into a royal court with green festoons
The banks of dark lagoons.

In the deep heart of every forest tree
The blood is all aglee,
And there's a look about the leafless bowers
As if they dreamed of flowers.

As yet the turf is dark, although you know
That, not a span below,
A thousand germs are groping through the gloom,
And soon will burst their tomb.

In gardens you may note amid the dearth,
The crocus breaking earth;
And near the snowdrop's tender white and green,
The violet in its screen.

But many gleams and shadows need must pass
Along the budding grass,
And weeks go by, before the enamored South
Shall kiss the rose's mouth.

Yet still on every side we trace the hand
Of winter in the land,
Save where the maple reddens on the lawn,
Flushed by the season's dawn;

Or where, like those strange semblances we find
That age to childhood bind,
The elm puts on, as if in nature's scorn,
The brown of autumn corn.

Still there's a sense of blossoms yet unborn
In the sweet airs of morn;
One almost looks to see the very street
Grow purple at his feet.

At times a fragrant breeze comes floating by,
And brings, you know not why,
A feeling as when eager crowds await
Before a palace gate

Some wondrous pageant; and you scarce would
   start,
If from a beech's heart,
A blue-eyed Dryad, stepping forth, should say,
"Behold me! I am May!"

Henry Timrod

Picture opposite
SOUTHERN MANSION
Ken Dequaine

April and May

April cold with dropping rain
Willows and lilacs brings again,
The whistle of returning birds,
And the trumpet-lowing of the herds.
The scarlet maple-keys betray
What potent blood hath modest May,
What fiery force the earth renews,
The wealth of forms, the flush of hues;
What joy in rosy waves outpoured
Flows from the heart of Love, the Lord.

Ralph Waldo Emerson

ACKNOWLEDGMENTS

AN EASTER GREETING TO EVERY CHILD WHO LOVES "ALICE" (Supplement to Alice in Wonderland) by Lewis Carroll. Harper & Row, Publishers. THE MARIPOSA LILY by Ina Donna Coolbrith. From: THE POETRY OF NATURE by Charles G. D. Roberts. Houghton, Mifflin & Company, Publishers. EASTER EGG BREAD; FROSTED EASTER ROLLS: KULICH (RUSSIAN EASTER CAKE) Recipes from THE COUNTRY BREAD COOKBOOK by Darlene Kronschnabel, Copyright © 1978 by Darlene Kronschnabel, published by Ideals Publishing Corporation. AN EASTER CAROL by Christina G. Rossetti. From: SING-SONG by Christina G. Rossetti, published by Macmillan Publishing Co., Inc.

The Rhodora

Lines on Being Asked, Whence Is the Flower?

In May, when sea-winds pierced our solitudes,
I found the fresh rhodora in the woods,
Spreading its leafless blooms in a damp nook,
To please the desert and the sluggish brook;
The purple petals fallen in the pool
Made the black waters with their beauty gay;
Here might the red-bird come his plumes to cool,
And court the flower that cheapens his array.
Rhodora! if the sages ask thee why
This charm is wasted on the marsh and sky,
Dear, tell them that if eyes were made for seeing,
Then beauty is its own excuse for being.
Why thou wert there, O rival of the rose!
I never thought to ask; I never knew,
But in my simple ignorance suppose
The self-same Power that brought me there
   brought you.

Ralph Waldo Emerson

It's Our
40th Birthday!
IDEALS 1944-1984

You won't want to miss a single issue of our Anniversary Year! Join us in celebrating Mother's Day and springtime in our next issue.

Mother's Day Ideals is a colorful observance of the traditional holiday in honor of women everywhere. Explore with us the world of women — mothers, daughters, aunts, and nieces who have succeeded in their lives. Share a look at "Noteworthy Women in History" and "Mothers of Famous Men and Women." Enjoy the new "Readers' Reflections" pages which feature poetry and amusing anecdotes from our readers. Interesting articles, delightful prose, and nostalgic poetry accompany vivid color photographs and artwork.

An Ideals gift subscription for family and friends, beginning with our Mother's Day issue, is the perfect way to share a world of beauty year round.